Praise for The Success Tax Shuffle

"The Success Tax Shuffle is a must read for anyone who has accumulated significant assets. It provides a well described and understandable host of solutions that can provide many different options to solving the issues that we face in passing wealth to the next generation."

Steve Meehan
Chairman
Bellwether Investment Management Inc.

"Death and taxes may be inevitable, but Bill's book "The Success Tax Shuffle" is a must read for any individual that is fortunate enough to have built up a nest egg. Success Tax is real and can be minimized with the steps set out in this book. At the end of the day, we all want to pass the wealth we have created in our lifetime to those who we love and the endeavors that are important to us, this book can make sure that happens."

Chris S. Reynolds
President and CEO
Investment Planning Counsel Inc.

"Imagine working so hard all your life, only to have a big chunk of your estate taken away from the people you had intended it for. This is a reality that so many Canadians have faced and will continue to face — unless they plan for the "success tax" that Bill Green explains so clearly in this book. It's a must-read for anyone who wants to preserve the wealth they've worked so hard to build."

Marjo Johne
Toronto freelance writer and regular contributor to The Globe and Mail Report on Business section

"Bills book is an excellent read in gaining an understanding of the tax liability associated with one's financial success. Without resorting to jargon he explains things in easy to understand language for the reader whether financially experienced or not. A worthy addition to any financial planning library."

John Welch
Senior Wealth Consultant - Cidel Asset Management Inc.

The Success
TAX SHUFFLE

How to stop CRA

from becoming one of your

biggest beneficiaries!

William (Bill) Green

CFP®, FMA, FDS, CIM®

Green, William Edward 1963 –
The Success Tax Shuffle®

ISBN 978-0-9951647-0-3
Fifth edition July 18th, 2017

1235181 Ontario Inc.
120 Milton St., Bracebridge, ON
P1L 2G4
wegreen@billgreen.ca

Disclaimer

The tax rates, tax credits, tax deductions, and examples used in this book are rounded to make the examples easier to understand. Your personal tax implications will depend on your particular situation and could be less than or greater than the examples used in this book. The ideas expressed in this book are my own and do not necessarily reflect those of any company or business that I may have a business relationship with. The people, company names, and situations described in the examples in this book are fictional and do not represent any actual persons or companies. Always seek legal, accounting, investment and financial planning advice before implementing any actions or ideas found in this book.

Dedication

This book is dedicated to all the clients, co-workers and business partners that I have had the privilege of working within the financial planning industry over the last 25 years. With special thanks to MMM for giving me the encouragement and the push I needed to finally put my financial and estate planning knowledge into writing.

Contents

The Success Tax Shuffle®

Introduction

In order to understand what The Success Tax Shuffle is you first need to know what the Success Tax is. Many people have never heard of the Success Tax, and there is an excellent reason for that. The main reason being, that there is not an official tax called the Success Tax in Canada. However, that doesn't mean that the Success Tax does not exist. I assure you it does. It is just known by other names.

There are only two things in life that are certain; Death and Taxes. While each of these is bad enough on its own, when combined it's a double whammy. Just at a time when your family is likely at its most vulnerable, and possibly in need of emotional and financial support, they could be dealing with the government and paying the biggest tax bill they will ever see.

The Success Tax that I am referring to is the tax that we pay if we are successful in our investing and have assets that are going to be taxable when sold or when deemed to have been sold. That's right, you do not actually have to sell something to trigger the tax. You could be considered to have sold it when ownership of the asset changes hands, even if you do not get any money from the sale. This deemed sale happens upon your death or when you change ownership of a taxable asset.

The Success Tax takes one of two forms. The first form is deferred taxation on registered products such as RSPs, GRSPs, LRSPs, RIFs, LIFs and other similar retirement tax-sheltered vehicles. The second form of the Success Tax is the tax on deferred Capital Gains. This tax effects such assets as stocks, mutual funds, art, antiques, collectibles, real estate, private businesses and sometimes even bonds. While there is no hiding from the Success Tax, there are several things that can be done to help legally reduce or even eliminate the amount that your estate or your heirs pay.

The Success Tax shuffle is not a way of avoiding taxes that are legally due, nor is it a donation tax scheme. The Success Tax Shuffle is the process of arranging your assets and affairs in order to take advantage of the current tax laws, tax credits, deductions and other estate planning tools with a view to reducing or even eliminating the Success Tax. This will allow more of your hard earned assets to go to those you love and not those you love to hate.

This book is meant to act as a guide to enlighten, educate and otherwise inform the reader, as most people are genuinely unaware of just how the Success Tax will affect their estate and their heirs, and to encourage the reader to seek professional guidance. This book is not meant to be a do it yourself guide, as tax and estate planning is a very complex and personal issue.

Your situation, while it may be similar to someone else's, is unique to you and your family. You should always consult with your personal financial planner, accountant and legal professional before implementing any tax or estate planning strategies.

I have been a financial planner for over 25 years and have seen many well-intentioned people make some pretty big and costly mistakes while following the advice of their friends, relatives or with a little knowledge gained from a book or the news media. Some people will not seek help as they feel it will cost them to do so; believe me, when I tell you it could cost you, your estate and your heirs a whole lot more if you get it wrong.

Chapter 1

Just What Is The Success Tax?

As mentioned in the introduction to this book, there really is not a tax called the Success Tax, at least not in Canada, but rather it is a combination of two other forms of taxation on assets that delay annual taxation. If you have been successful with investing and asset accumulation then you are bound to be affected by these taxes; the more successful you have been, the greater the potential for a larger Success Tax.

The first form of the Success Tax is the tax on deferred retirement asset plans. These plans include retirement savings accounts such as Registered Retirement Plans, personal and spousal plans (RRSPs, SRSP), Group Retirement Savings Plans (GRSPs), Defined Contribution Pension Plans (DCPPs) and Locked-in Retirement Accounts (LIRAs), assets that were once in a Pension Plan, Retirement Income Funds (RIFs) and Life Income Funds (LIFs), to name a few. The exception in this group is a Tax Free Savings Account (TFSA); TFSA accounts are currently exempt from any form of taxation.

The second form of the Success Tax is the deferred or unrealized capital gains tax on capital assets. This includes any item that you have purchased for one price and sell or are deemed to have sold for a higher price. These items are subject to the capital gains tax when the item is sold, or ownership is changed. The types of assets that could be affected by this form of the Success Tax include stocks, mutual funds, art, antiques, collectibles, real estate, private businesses, and sometimes bonds. The exception in this group is your principal residence. More on that later.

The Success Tax could affect you when there is a change of ownership on these assets. That change of ownership happens automatically when you die, or if you gift or transfer an asset to another person.

Chapter 2
Tax-Deferred Growth

Both registered plans and unrealized capital gains allow you to grow your assets faster and to larger amounts than you could if these items were subject to annual taxation. This is due to the tax-deferred growth these items offer. Tax-deferred growth allows more of your assets to remain invested and compound on a tax-deferred basis. While this is great when you are building your assets, the greater your tax deferral, the greater your Success Tax liability is likely to be. As they say, there are only two certainties in life, Death and Taxes, and the taxes will eventually become due.

The Success Tax kicks in when you dispose of or otherwise change ownership of an asset that has a deferred tax liability. This happens regardless of how the ownership is changed, via gift, sale or death. The tax man wants his share. When you die you are deemed to have sold everything you own just prior to your death. This happens regardless of the existence of joint ownership or beneficiary designations. Joint ownership and beneficiary designations help you reduce or eliminate probate fees, but they do not eliminate the Success Tax. Note: The Success Tax on registered assets can be deferred under certain situations. More on this later.

Chapter 3

Success Tax Calculation

Upon death, you are deemed to have disposed of all of your assets just before you died. This disposal or change of ownership is a taxable event. The taxable amount depends on the asset and is either 100% of the value of the account, as is the case with registered assets, or for capital assets it is the taxable gain that has occurred to the asset since you acquired it. So your personal Success Tax will depend on how successful you have been on deferring taxes and building your assets. The more successful you have been, the greater your Success Tax liability is going to be.

The tax due is calculated as the taxable amount or taxable gain on your assets multiplied by your tax rate at the time of sale or change of ownership, which as I stated occurs automatically upon your death. The price used in calculating the value of your assets is the fair market value of the assets. The fair market value or FMV is determined by either the public markets, in the case of publicly traded assets, or a price determined by the executor/executrix of your estate for non-publicly traded assets. The values used can be challenged by Canada Revenue Agency (CRA) if they feel they are too low. Therefore, your executor/executrix needs to have a sound means of calculating the value and must be able to prove their value is fair if challenged by CRA.

The amount that is taxable depends on a few things. As I mentioned with registered plans, the taxable amount is 100% of the value of the accounts. With capital assets, the taxable amount is the difference between the FMV and the adjusted cost base or ACB. The ACB is the price you paid for the asset, plus certain additional expenses incurred during the time you owned the asset.

With registered plans the total value of these tax-deferred plans is fully taxable regardless of the assets that are held within these plans, i.e. cash investments held in personal non-registered accounts are not affected by the Success Tax. However, cash investments held inside of registered plans are fully taxable. Stocks or other equity type investments held in a non-registered account qualify as capital gains assets, where only the growth is taxable, but when held inside of a registered plan, 100% of the value is taxable. More on this later in the chapter on capital assets.

When everything you own is sold, and the value is added to your final tax return, the government that has been patiently waiting to get their hands on your money will get their share. How big that share is, is somewhat up to you. If you have put plans in place to reduce or eliminate the Success Tax, you may be able to reduce, or even eliminate this final tax grab.

You may not care, once you are gone, that a huge portion of your estate could go to the government in the form of taxes. You should, however, at least know just how much of your hard-earned assets the government could be getting, and what your options are, before you allow your heirs to hand it over to the tax man, without so much as a second thought.

Chapter 4

Registered Plans

Most registered plans have one thing in common, and that is that they all defer taxation until some later point in time when the money eventually has to come out of them. The exception to the rule here is a Tax Free Savings Account or TFSA, as these plans do not attract any taxation and are currently exempt from the Success Tax.

While you are adding to your tax-deferred plans, you are reducing your taxation at the time and are deferring the tax to a later date. Tax deferral is a great thing and adds to the value of your savings, but eventually the taxes must be paid. When you take out small amounts from these plans as income, you pay tax on what you take out. The balance continues to grow tax-free. This allows you to reduce or control your annual taxation; however, by delaying withdrawals you may be increasing your total lifetime taxation.

Since our tax system in Canada is progressive, the more money you make, the more tax you pay. If you were to cash out all of your retirement plans in a lump sum, as you are forced to do upon death, the entire amount of all of your plans would then be added to your income for that year, and would become fully taxable. With a spousal rollover this tax can be delayed, but not eliminated.

A beneficiary designation does not remove this tax liability; it only delays the liability, and only if the account has a named beneficiary who is a spouse, common-law partner or a dependent child. Having this type of beneficiary designation allows the total value of your plans to be transferred to the qualified beneficiary and for the plan to maintain its tax deferred status until such time as the beneficiary removes the money from the plan. This delays the collection of the Success Tax; it does not eliminate it. Since it is usually only your spouse or common-law partner who qualifies for this type of transfer, the only way of avoiding the Success Tax on your registered plans is to leave them to your spouse and then to have that spouse remarry when you die and leave the assets to the new spouse and to repeat the process until all the money is spent. Not really a practical strategy.

As an example if you had $1,000,000 in your registered plans when you passed away, and no spouse or dependent children, the tax could be as high as 50% or $500,000. It does not matter how much growth has occurred in these plans as 100% of the value of the accounts are taxable. More detailed examples follow later in this book.

Does this possible 50% tax payment mean that you would have been better off not accumulating assets in a tax-deferred plan in the first place? No, it does not. Tax-deferred plans allow your assets to grow faster and to larger amounts than if you had to pay annual taxation on these investments. As long as registered plans are used in the correct way, these plans are a great financial planning tool.

Tax-deferred plans are for long term savings, not short term savings. In order for the tax deferral of a registered plan to work, a couple of things need to happen. First off, the money needs time to grow tax-free over a number of years, or when you take the money out your tax rate needs to be lower than it was when you put it in. The tax-deferred growth can still work even if your tax rate is not lower when you take the funds out, as long as it has had enough time to grow and compound tax-free. You will not need as much time for tax-deferred growth if your tax rate is lower when you take the funds out compared to what it was when you put the funds in. However, if your tax rate is higher when you withdraw the funds, you will need time for the magic of tax-free compounding growth to work for you.

Due to the high rate of the Success Tax on your estate, there can be an argument made for taking more money out of your registered plans than required by tax regulations as you age, even if you do not need to spend the funds. If your tax rate is lower in any particular year than it is likely to be in the future, then it might make sense to take some extra funds out of your registered plans and to reinvest them in either your TFSA or a non-registered account. This would allow you to take advantage of the lower tax rate and to reduce your Success Tax and your total lifetime taxation. Please be sure to consult with your financial planner before implementing this strategy as there are other items and factors to be considered, such as the Old Age Security

(OAS) clawback and the annual taxation of the funds outside of the registered plan.

Chapter 5
Capital Assets

As mentioned, taxable capital assets are those assets that you have purchased or acquired for one price and that have increased in value above the adjusted cost base or ACB. The gain is usually taxable as a capital gain once the asset is sold or ownership is changed or upon the death of the owner. Capital assets include stocks, mutual funds, art, antiques, collectibles, real estate, private businesses and sometimes bonds.

Capital gains taxes were introduced in 1972; prior to that, there was no tax on capital gains in Canada. From 1972 until 1992 in the case of real estate and until 1994 in the case of equities we all had a $100,000 capital gains exemption, meaning that we could each make $100,000 of capital gains tax-free. This no longer applies. Therefore, some of the things our parents and grandparents were able to do tax-free, like gifting the cottage to you without paying any tax, are now taxable events.

Now that capital gains are taxable, any increase in the value of your capital assets since you acquired them, or since the assets value on December 31, 1971 (if you have owned it that long), are taxable as a capital gain. There is still a capital gains exemption for certain small business shares, farm property or fishing property. However, most everyday investments do not qualify for this exemption.

At the time of writing, in our current tax system, capital gains are 50% tax-free. This means that if you have a $500,000 capital gain, $250,000 of those gains would be tax-free and $250,000 would be taxable at your marginal tax rate. If your tax rate is 50% then on a $250,000 taxable capital gain, you or your estate would owe $125,000 in taxes, or 25% of the total gain. While 25% tax is much better than the 50% on registered plans we saw earlier, it is still a big chunk of your hard earned assets that are going to pay taxes.

This 25% can sometimes be a bigger problem to the estate than the 50% on registered plans, depending on where the gain has occurred and the liquidity of the asset or assets with the gain. Often capital assets such as the family business, rental properties, the family cottage, art, antiques and collectibles are illiquid or have sentimental attachments. Therefore, the cash needed to pay the tax may not be readily available to the estate, without selling the precious family asset.

This can lead to a couple of problems. First, emotionally it may be difficult for the family to sell an asset that has been in the family for many years, particularly at a time when they are also dealing with the recent passing of a loved one.

The second issue could be the price that the estate can get for the asset if cash is needed quickly to pay the taxes. The estate may not be able to get a fair price for the asset, based on an estate or fire sale price. This sometimes happens because when items need to be sold quickly the price one can ask is often lower than the price one could get if they could afford to take their time to sell the item. For example, a family business may need to be sold quickly in order to keep things running and in good order. A family cottage may need to be sold quickly if no one is available to look after it or maintain it. Items may just need to be sold quickly as the executor/executrix and the heirs want to be able to move on with their lives. As you can see, there are many reasons why a quick sale, below market value, can happen.

While a lower price will mean a lower tax bill, selling an asset below its fair market value is not usually a great tax planning strategy. Also, the CRA could challenge any numbers that are below fair market value (FMV). For tax purposes, capital assets have to be recorded as being sold at their FMV or a price that a willing buyer would pay.

While you can gift or sell an asset for any price, the price recorded on your income tax return has to be the FMV. Often parents will transfer ownership of a property to a loved one for a token sum; however, if the asset has a taxable gain this does not eliminate the tax liability. In fact, selling property to a loved one below the FMV to try and avoid taxation or land transfer fees can incur double taxation if not done correctly.

Let's look at an example where gifting an asset could cause double taxation. Say you owned a cottage that had an ACB of $250,000 and a FMV of $1,000,000. If you were to sell the family cottage to one of your children for a dollar or gift it to them for love and affection, the land transfer deed would show a purchase price of $1. With a non-arm's length sale (meaning a sale to someone that is related to you) of taxable assets, the CRA will deem that the sale took place at FMV. Therefore, they would deem that you had sold the asset for its FMV or for $1,000,000. You would still have a $750,000 gain, of which $375,000 would be taxable. At a 50% tax rate you would owe $187,500 in taxes even though you did not actually get any funds from the sale.

The double taxation occurs if the property is not your children's Principal Residence and they dispose of the cottage. As the price that they paid is recorded as $1 and since the FMV is $1,000,000 this would mean that they could instantly have a $999,999 capital gain, $250,000 of which was never taxable and a $749,999 gain that you have already paid taxes on. All because you wanted to save some money on land transfer fees.

Chapter 6
When Is The Success Tax Due?

Upon your death your chosen executor/executrix has six months or until April 30th of the following year (whichever period is greater) to file your final personal tax return and pay the taxes that are due. Your estate or a trust set up by your will can continue to exist and file annual tax returns beyond this period. However, your final tax return and the taxes due have to be dealt with pretty quickly after your passing. Usually, the taxes have to be paid in full at the time the final return is filed. Under certain circumstances, your estate can elect to pay the taxes over a period of time with interest if the estate had certain capital assets or has filed a rights and things return.

Should your estate not be able to liquidate assets during this period of time, a fair market value will have to be determined and used for the purposes of estate settlement. If the value that the assets are finally sold for is different than the original amount used on your final personal return, then an adjustment can be made to the estate return.

Also upon your death, your estate is likely to have to deal with probate fees or Estate Administration Tax (EAT) as it is called in Ontario. These are fees that are charged by your provincial government in order to process and validate a Will and the transfer of the estate's assets to the heirs and beneficiaries. These fees vary from province to province and range from a minimum of $0 to as high as 1.5% of the value of the assets that require probate. In this book I will use 1.5% in our examples, currently the highest fee, which is in Ontario, for any assets over $50,000. I will use this high fee so that you can see just how little these charges are when compared to the Success Tax. So when looking at the examples remember that the probate fees saved, in fact, are likely a lot less than those quoted.

Arranging your estate to minimize or avoid probate fees can be a great way to save some money; however, probate fees should not be the only consideration, as some tactics used to avoid probate can actually cause costlier problems than the probate fees you are trying to avoid.

Chapter 7
Exempt Items

Some items do not attract the Success Tax when they are sold, deemed sold, or otherwise transferred to someone else. These exempt items include any items that are subject to annual taxation, this includes non-tax sheltered plans or items that do not have a deferred taxable gain attached to them, such as Cash, Bank Accounts, GICs, and Savings Bonds. Since you pay tax on any growth on these items annually there is no deferred tax liability.

Four other items that are exempt from annual taxation and the Success tax are Tax Free Savings Accounts (TFSAs, *regardless of the assets held inside of the account),* the cash value of exempt life insurance contracts, Life Insurance proceeds and your Principal Residence *(see chapter 8).*

Just because these items are not subject to the Success Tax does not mean that you should only hold or invest in assets that are exempt from the Success Tax. The tax-deferred growth and often higher long-term rates of return that can be achieved by investing in, and holding, assets that are affected by the Success Tax is well worth the extra tax you will have to pay in the long run. After all, it is better to have a large Success

Tax bill and a big estate, than it is to have no assets, no estate, and no Success Tax.

Chapter 8
Home Sweet Home

As I mentioned in Chapter 7, your Principal Residence is one item that is exempt from the Success Tax. Many people, however, do not understand how this exemption works and can often run into problems when they own more than one property at a time.

Currently, we are allowed one tax-free principal residence per tax filing couple at a time, based on the Principal Residence Exemption offered by Canada Revenue Agency. This exemption states that one house that we own and use for personal use can be classified as our Principal Residence. If it meets the requirements in the guidelines then any growth on this property will be tax-free when the property is sold, deemed sold or otherwise transferred to someone else. In the past there was either no tax on capital gains or there was an exemption that helped reduce or eliminate the taxes, so our parents and grandparents were not as affected by the Success Tax as the generations that follow are going to be.

The Principal residence exemption rule generally states that if the property is "Ordinarily inhabited" by the owner or a family member, and is not used to generate taxable income, that the land and the buildings on the land are not excessive for personal use, and that the land is required for personal use of the property, then the exemption applies. Let's say you had a house on a 100-acre plot of land, you would only be exempt on the value of the house and a small portion of the land (generally about 1.25 of an acre) but not on all of the land. A portion of the gain in the value of the land would be taxable.

The property you claim as your principal residence can be a second property, such as a cabin, cottage or vacation home. However, you can only claim one property at a time. If you own more than one property at a time then CRA form T2019(IND) (Estates use T1255) is used for claiming the exemption, and calculating the taxable gain. This form uses an averaging formula to calculate the taxable amount based on the total holding period of both properties. As of October 3rd, 2016 you are now required to report the sale or change of use of any property you own, either on a Schedule 3 or on a T2019.

Despite what many people do and think, you cannot legally move into your second property and claim it as a Principal Residence for any growth that occurred before you moved into that property, if you have already claimed the growth on another property over the same period of time.

Many people get caught on this when they own property in the city and a cottage at the same time. In retirement, they will often sell the house in the city and move into the cabin or cottage. Upon the sale of the city property, they do not claim the sale of the property in the city as a capital gain, (Prior to the 2016 income tax year reporting the sale of a Principal residence was not a requirement, it is now required.)

therefore by default the sale of the city property used the Principal Residence exemption for the time period for which both properties were jointly owned.

When they move into the cottage, it becomes their principal residence, but only on a go-forward basis. Therefore, any gain that had occurred before they moved and sold the other Principal Residence property, the city home by default in this case, becomes a taxable capital gain. The gain is not due until you sell your new principal residence, however the total gain will be averaged using the formula on form T2091(IND) or T2155.

In the past many people did not claim this gain and assume that it was not an issue. Often the problem is not discovered until the cottage property is sold, deemed sold or transferred to someone else via the estate years later. When this happens, it can be very difficult, and costly, to figure out the correct amount of tax due and often it gets misreported, overstated or deductions are disallowed by CRA.

Many people have gotten away with not claiming the gains on second properties, as it was very difficult for these gains to be tracked. That has all changed with the switch to electronic property registry. Now in most places every sale or change of ownership is recorded electronically, and it can easily be tracked and matched up to reported capital gains. Therefore, going forward this will likely become a much bigger issue than it has been in the past. CRA is monitoring third party information about property sales and now with the requirement to report the sale of your Principal residence on your income tax return, it is just a matter of time, before we start hearing about audits in this area.

Please note as of the 2016 income tax year you are now required to report the sale of your Principal residence on your income tax return, if you own just one property you can use Schedule 3 and claim the exemption. If you own more than one property you may have to use form T2091(IND) and average the gains.

Chapter 9

Know Before You Go

As mentioned, you may not care that once you are gone that a significant portion of your hard-earned assets are going to go to pay taxes, instead of going to those you care about. You should at least know the estimated amounts that could be lost to taxes and what options you may have. After all, you have likely tried very hard to minimize or avoid taxes most of your life, so if you do not like paying taxes while you're alive, then you should at least take the time to find out how to minimize the taxes your heirs will have to pay when you are gone.

Many people simply say, "Well I will be gone, so I don't care." These same individuals are often shocked when they find out just how much of their hard-earned estate will not go to those they love, but rather to pay taxes. We all pay taxes. Without taxes our governments and social programs could not function, so I am not against paying taxes. However, there is no reason to pay more than your fair share, and you have every right to structure your affairs in such a way as to minimize the amount of tax that you pay during your lifetime and upon your death.

Please note that unless you have a large outstanding income tax bill your estate will never owe more in taxes than the value of your assets. So if your estate owes taxes, it has the money or the assets with which to pay those taxes. Plus, you know that the government will put your hard earned money to good use, right?

Many people are aware of probate fees and will often go to great lengths to avoid paying these fees; these same people are often totally unaware of the Success Tax and the much larger bite that it is going to take out of their estates. Probate fees are a maximum of 1.5% of your estate while the Success tax could be up to 50% of the value of some of your assets, therefore arranging your affairs to reduce probate fees should not be your biggest concern.

Often people are totally shocked once they estimate just what their Success Tax could be. Once they find out most people will take steps to do what they can to minimize or even eliminate this final tax grab. If you want to get an estimate of just what your Success Tax might be you can visit www.yoursuccesstax.ca and use the online calculator to find out.

Chapter 10

Sample Success Tax Calculation

The Success Tax calculator worksheet on the next page is broken down into four sections: Registered Products, Cottage/Second Property, Equity Investments, and the Totals section.

The sample Success Tax calculator on the next page can be found online at http://www.yoursuccesstax.ca

Your Success Tax Estimate

REGISTERED PRODUCTS (RRSP, Etc)

Current Value of Your Accounts	$ 1,000,000.00
Current Value Partners Accounts	$
Other:	$
Other:	$
Total of above	$ 1,000,000.00

COTTAGE/SECOND PROPERTY

Current Fair Market Value of Second Property(s)	$ 1,000,000.00
Adjusted Cost base of above Property(s)	$ 250,000.00
Capital Gain on Property(s)	$ 750,000.00
50% Of Above	$ 375,000.00

EQUITY INVESTMENTS

Mutual Funds/Stocks/Business Interests/Other	$ 1,000,000.00
Adjusted Cost base of above	$ 250,000.00
Capital Gain on Equities	$ 750,000.00
50% Of Above	$ 375,000.00

TOTALS

Total from Registered Plan Section	$ 1,000,000.00
Total from Second Property Section	$ 375,000.00
Total from Equity Section	$ 375,000.00
Total of above	$ 1,750,000.00
Estimated Success Tax Rate	50.00%
Total Success Tax Due	**$875,000.00**

In the registered products section, you would enter the current or estimated future value of any assets that are 100% fully taxable upon withdrawal or deregistration. This includes all registered assets mentioned in Chapter 4. In this example, we are just using an RRSP. The $1,000,000 RRSP is subject to full taxation, just as it would be if you cashed it out while you are still alive. The RRSP may be able to roll over to a spouse, common-law partner or a dependent child, as long as they have been named as beneficiary This roll over would delay the Success tax until that person removes the money from the plan, it will not eliminate the tax liability.

In the Cottage/Second Property section, you would enter all real estate holdings, with the exception of your Principal Residence (See Chapter 8). In this example, we are using a $1,000,000 cottage or second property, that has a $250,000 adjusted cost base. Real estate property is usually considered a capital asset, meaning that the growth is taxed as a capital gain. Therefore, $750,000 is taxable as a capital gain. Since capital gains are currently 50% tax-free only $375,000 will be subject to the Success Tax.

In the Equity Investments section, you would enter all equity type investments that are not held inside of a Registered product, such as an RRSP or a TFSA. In this example we are using $1,000,000 of an equity-based non-registered investment account, that has an adjusted cost base of $250,000. Since equity investments are considered capital assets, only the gain is taxable. On the $750,000 gain, $375,000 is taxable and subject to the Success Tax. Stocks, mutual funds, art, antiques, collectibles, and private businesses that are subject to the Success Tax should be entered in this section as well.

The Totals section summarizes the taxable amounts from each of the three different sections and, using a sample 50% tax rate, estimates the amount of the Success Tax. In this example, there is $875,000 worth of taxes due on $3,000,000 worth of assets. Your personal Success Tax rate will depend on the total value of your estate. Given the fact that all your taxable assets are added to your final return, it is very likely that your Success Tax rate will be the highest rate attributable in your province.

Chapter 11
Estate Planning 101

Wills, beneficiary designations, joint ownership and charitable donations are all great ways to minimize or even eliminate the Success Tax. In general terms the following information can help with your Success Tax planning. I cannot, however, get into specific ways that these techniques can be used to reduce or eliminate your personal Success Tax.

Proper tax and estate planning require a personalized and unique strategy for you and your family. Therefore, you need to work with a qualified financial planner or estate planner who will work with you, your family, your lawyer, your accountant and your investment planner to come up with a personal success tax savings plan that works best for you and your family.

Wills

The first step is to make sure that you actually have a valid Will or Wills. Yes, under certain circumstances, you can have more than one valid Will. Many people either do not have a valid Will, or they have a Will that doesn't accurately reflect their wishes. I cannot tell you the number of times I have read someone's Will and then explained it back to them in simple terms, only to have them say, "Well that's not what I want."

Once you are gone, the only legal means that you have is what is written down in your Will or a Trust you have set up. Your heirs cannot legally act on some items that you may have personally told them you wanted dealt with in a certain way if it is not written that way in the Will, or if the Will says something different than what you told them. Once you are gone, your Will needs to lay out your intentions clearly, so you need to make sure that this is looked after while you are still capable of making a Will.

In my opinion, a Will should always be written with the help of your lawyer, and reviewed and updated on a regular basis. While handwritten Wills and Will kits are legal, and the initial cost is less expensive than a lawyer, the overall cost can be much higher. I have seen many costly problems arise from mistakes and misinterpretations of handwritten Wills and Will Kits. They could have been easily avoided with a proper Will. Note: You should also get your lawyer to do your Power of Attorneys (POA) or Personal Care Directives (PCD) at the same time as they are making up your Will. POA or PCD documents, sometimes called a Living Will, allow an appointed person or persons to take certain actions on your behalf legally while you are alive but unable or incapable of looking after your own health or financial affairs. However, these documents become void upon death so you still require a Will.

Your Will also needs to be updated when certain life events occur, such as marriage, addition or change of a common law partner, divorce, birth of a child/grandchild, change of financial situation, or with the loss of an heir or beneficiary, just to name a few. Note: while a marriage will usually void an existing will, a divorce does not. It is imperative to keep your Will updated based on the changes that happen in your lifetime.

Beneficiary Designations

Certain financial products such as Registered Investments and Insurance Products can have beneficiaries assigned to them, allowing these assets to pass to the named beneficiaries outside of your Will; this allows the items to transfer privately and without the requirement to go through the probate process and avoids the probate fee.

While Registered or Insurance assets with named beneficiaries may be able to pass to your heirs outside of your estate, this does not avoid the Success Tax due on these assets. Sometimes, if it is not handled properly, naming beneficiaries on these plans can, in fact, create bigger problems for the estate with estate equalization and liquidity inside of the estate. The estate owes the tax on the asset, not the heir; however, the estate may not have the cash with which to pay the taxes if the money has already been transferred directly to a beneficiary. Getting money back from a beneficiary can be like getting a bone back from a dog: sometimes it is easy sometimes it is not.

Life insurance proceeds are exempt from the Success Tax; however, naming a beneficiary on an insurance policy other than the estate means that the money is not available to the estate to be used to pay taxes, make donations or otherwise distribute according to the Will. Naming the estate as a beneficiary on an insurance product means that probate will be charged on the value of the policy. If the plan is to use the proceeds to pay taxes, make tax deductible donations, or follow directions in the Will, it may well be worth paying the probate fee on any insurance assets in order to have access to the funds inside of the estate.

Joint Ownership

Having assets in joint names is a strategy that is often used to avoid probate, but joint ownership can cause problems if it is not used carefully and correctly. These problems can be far costlier than the small amount of probate fees that you are trying to avoid.

Joint ownership like a named beneficiary allows assets to pass outside of an estate and to avoid probate. Using joint ownership does not avoid the Success Tax. In fact, a change to joint ownership can actually trigger the Success Tax and taxes could be due even if no cash changed hands at the time the joint owners name was added to the asset.

Adding someone else's name to your assets before you are ready to actually hand them over can get complicated and costly. Once you add someone else's name to your asset it at least partly becomes their asset, meaning it could be subject to their creditors, their spouse, their death, and their greed, to name just a few issues that could arise.

If a joint owner ends up claiming bankruptcy or getting a divorce, the asset that you put into their name could form part of their assets, their estate or in the case of a divorce their net family property. If this happens, you could find that your new co-owner is not someone you would have picked, such as your son's or your daughter's ex-partner. If you wanted or needed your asset back you could end up having to buy it back, even though you gave it away in the first place.

Do not think for a minute that greed could not happen to your family; it can happen to almost any family. I cannot tell you the number of times I have seen and heard of parents gifting assets either by joint ownership or inside their Will. They were sure that the child would do what they wanted and distribute the assets according to their wishes, or return the asset to them if they wanted it back. However, the child has said "No, that is mine" and has refused to allow a change of ownership without being compensated for returning the asset or has declined to share or change ownership of an asset with their siblings as the parent had requested. In short, if it is not listed in the Will, or a trust you have no control over it beyond the grave, and only limited control if the asset is held jointly.

If your children ever fought over a piece of chocolate cake or a toy when they were younger, imagine what it could be like if it were over money. Regrettably, I have seen family members end their relationships over what often amounts to a minuscule part of an estate all because they disagree with something as small as mom's jewelry, dad's tools, a piece of artwork, a family heirloom or what a particular asset is worth. In the end, despite what we would like to think, it often comes down to money and material possessions.

Another issue with joint ownership is that your financial situation could change and you might need the asset or assets back for one reason or another, maybe to sell to cover your expenses. However, the new joint owner could refuse to allow you to regain control over the assets held jointly. You say your kids would not do that to you. Sadly, I have seen it happen more than once where the parents were sure it would not be an issue. Sometimes it is not your children, but rather their partners or their situations that can cause the issues.

Remember, by adding someone else's name to your assets you are legally transferring ownership or partial ownership of that asset to that other person. This means that these joint assets are now subject to all the risks that the other party could face, such as bankruptcy, death, divorce, greed, and taxation.

Let's start with bankruptcy. If the new joint owner ends up in bankruptcy, the assets that you transferred to them could be subject to seizure and used to pay back their creditors.

Should the new joint owner die, the assets that you transferred could be dealt with by their Will. You could find yourself with a new partner at best, or being forced to buy back the asset to settle their estate or to regain control of your asset.

If the person you added as a joint owner gets divorced, you could find that your assets now form part of their divorce proceeds, and you could lose part of your assets in their divorce.

If the joint owner's situation changes or they simply get greedy and decide that they want to use the assets you transferred to them for their own use, you could lose control and not be able to get the assets back into your own name if required.

As mentioned, by adding a joint owner's name to your assets, you could trigger the tax at the time the joint owner's name is added and you could pay a much larger tax bill than the probate fees that you are trying to avoid.

As you can see, there are many reasons where joint ownership can be a precarious option. Make sure you fully understand all the possible risks and put plans in place to protect yourself if you go this route.

Trusts

A trust can be used as an estate planning tool and is a separate legal entity from the person that contributed the assets to the trust, the beneficiaries, and the trustee. This can be an excellent way to protect your assets from creditors, spouses or spendthrift children. A trust can be set up in your Will or beforehand. If used correctly and all, or almost all, possible outcomes are thoroughly thought out, then a trust can be an excellent solution to some estate issues. With recent changes to the taxation of trusts, tax savings are no longer the main advantages to a trust.

A trust does not help you avoid the Success Tax. However, it might delay it. In fact, transferring assets to a trust may even trigger the Success Tax at the time the assets are moved to the trust, if not done correctly. Using a spousal trust or a common law trust should not trigger the Success Tax; it will delay it until a future date. Keep in mind that with some trusts, assets can only be held inside of the trust for 21 years, then without proper planning the trust is deemed to have disposed of its assets, and the Success Tax is due. The trust does have the option of transferring the asset to the beneficiary and further delaying the Success Tax until the death of the beneficiary.

Before going to the expense of setting up a trust make sure that you have talked to those who you will be naming beneficiaries and the trustees, as well as your financial planner. You do this to make sure everyone understands your thoughts, goals and objectives for the trust, and to ensure that this is a viable option for you and your estate.

Donations

Tax deductible charitable donations are a great way to make a difference in our society and reduce our taxes at the same time. While many of us make donations throughout our lifetimes, we often forget or are unaware that this can be an incredible estate planning tool.

Usually, you are only allowed to deduct up to 75% of your taxable income as a charitable donation, however, in the year of death, you are allowed to deduct up to 100% of the net taxable income on your final income tax return. If your donation is greater than 100% of your net taxable income on that final return, part of the donation can be carried back and used to reduce the taxes already paid in the previous tax year. Charitable donations are tax credits meaning that they only reduce income taxes paid or payable. If you do not owe any taxes, then a donation will not get you a refund.

If you are making a donation that is $25,000 or more, you may wish to consider using a Donor Advised Fund or a Family Foundation. With the increased popularity and reduced costs of Donor Advised Funds, the average person not only has the option of donating a lump sum directly to their favorite charity, but they can also set up a Donor Advised Fund that keeps on giving long after they are gone. Think of a Donor Advised Fund as a less expensive version of a Family Foundation.

A gift to a Donor Advised Fund gives you or your estate the charitable donation receipt at the time the contribution is made. With a donation to a Donor Advised Fund you or your estate claim a large charitable donation in one tax year, but remain in control of the funds and the annual donations. This allows for a much larger gift over time and more flexibility than a single donation. This is also a great way to get the next generation involved in the process. For more information about donor-advised funds or family foundations, please speak to your financial planner.

Donations made by your estate are not only an excellent way to help out your favorite charities, but they are also an excellent way to reduce the Success Tax.

Income Tax changes introduced in 2016 affect the taxation of investment returns inside of an estate, how charitable donations are treated, as well as the capital gains tax relief on the donation of certain capital assets. In order to get the maximum benefit, you want to make sure that your estate is set up as a Graduated Rate Estate (GRE) at the time of your passing, this will ensure that your estate pays the least amount of tax, legally possible.

Chapter 12

The Success Tax Shuffle®

Now that you understand just what the Success Tax is, and how it is going to affect your estate, it is time to look at shuffling the deck more in your favor so that you can minimize the effects of the Success Tax and other estate planning pitfalls. The goal here is to make sure that your money is distributed in accordance with your wishes and desires and that as little as possible goes to the tax man.

The Success Tax shuffle is not a way of avoiding taxes that are legally due, nor is it a donation tax scheme. The Success Tax Shuffle is the process of arranging your assets and affairs in order to take advantage of the current tax laws, tax credits, deductions and other estate planning tools with a view to reduce or even eliminate the Success Tax so that your hard-earned assets go to those you love and not to places you prefer they not go.

The best way to illustrate the effects and costs of the Success Tax, as well as some of the common estate planning pitfalls, is going to be with some examples. Please note that tax rates and credits vary from province to province based on the amount of taxable income. Therefore, to keep things as simple as possible I have used an approximation of tax rates and credits. The amounts used are just examples. The Success Tax affects people at all levels of assets and investments. It doesn't matter if your Success Tax bill is going to be $8,750 or if it is going to be $87,500,000; the principals used in the Success Tax shuffle work the same.

Again to keep things simple and as easy to understand as possible, I am using one sample family for all examples and I will only change one or two things at a time. Please be sure to verify your personal tax rates and credits to confirm just how you and your estate will be affected by the Success Tax.

In these examples, I am going to assume that capital gains are 50% tax-free, although since this has changed several times over the years, there is no way of knowing for sure that this rate will remain the same when your Success Tax is eventually due. As well for a final income tax rate on all taxable assets I will be using a 50% rate to keep things simple. Your personal rate could of course be higher or lower.

Our Couple

I am going to use the fictitious couple Bob and Mary Smith and their family in our example: Bob Smith is 55 Years old, he is married to Mary Smith, who is 60, they live in Ontario. Bob and Mary have two grown children, Wendy, who is 30 and Paul, who is 35. Wendy is married to Dave and has two children. Paul is currently married to Donna, his second wife, and he has one child with his first wife Susan and one with Donna. Paul has creditor problems, and may be looking at claiming bankruptcy; however, Paul has hidden this from his parents and his sister. Only his current wife Donna knows this.

Bob works for ABC Manufacturing, a publicly traded company and he is set to retire in 5 years. Bob earns a salary of $175,000 a year.

Mary works for Alpha Research, a small private company. Mary also earns a salary of $175,000 a year.

Bob and Mary have a net worth of $6,000,000 *(see account breakdown on next page)* and no debt. Their assets are equally distributed between the two of them, in various holdings. Bob and Mary have written their Wills specifying that in the event they both pass away that Bob's assets go to Paul and that Mary's assets go to Wendy. In other words, the kids are to get $3,000,000 each, at least that is what Bob and Mary think.

Mary owns $1,000,000 of ABC stock inside of her TFSA that she purchased for $250,000. Bob holds $1,000,000 of ABC stock inside of his RRSP, which he paid $250,000 for, and he owns another $1,000,000 of ABC stock inside of his open nonregistered account, which he also purchased for $250,000. Bob and Mary bought both their house and their cottage at the same time in 1994 and spent $250,000 for their principal residence and $250,000 for the cottage. Very odd numbers but the point here is to illustrate how different items are affected by the Success Tax even though the purchase price and the market value are the same.

In each of our examples, I will assume that Bob and Mary both pass away at the same time and that their account values are the same in each example, and that they have no other taxable income in the year of death.

Smith Asset Details – Holdings & ACB

	Totals	ACB*	Holdings	Heir
Non-Registered Assets				
Mary's Open	1,000,000	1,000,000	Cash	Wendy
Bob's Open	1,000,000	250,000	ABC Stock	Paul
Total Non-Registered Assets	**2,000,000**	**1,250,000**		
Registered Assets				
Mary's TFSA	1,000,000	250,000	ABC Stock	Wendy
Bob's RRSP	1,000,000	250,000	ABC Stock	Paul
Total Registered Assets	**2,000,000**	**500,000**		
Personal Use Assets				
Principal Residence	1,000,000	250,000	Real estate	Wendy
Cottage	1,000,000	250,000	Real estate	Paul
Total Personal Use Assets	**2,000,000**	**500,000**		
Total Estate Assets	**6,000,000**	**2,250,000**		

*ACB
Mary's Open - ACB is equal to the FMV due to annual taxation
Bob's Open - $250,000 the price he paid plus any reinvested dividends
Mary's TFSA - TFSA is exempt from taxation
Bob's RRSP - $250,000 the price he paid plus any reinvested dividends
Principal Residence - Exempt from taxation
Cottage - $250,000 plus any major upgrades

Smith Asset Details – Taxable gains – Heirs

	Totals	Gain	Taxable*	Heir
Non-Registered Assets				
Mary's Open	1,000,000	N/A	0	Wendy
Bob's Open	1,000,000	750,000	375,000	Paul
Total Non-Registered Assets	**2,000,000**	**750,000**	**375,000**	
Registered Assets				
Mary's TFSA	1,000,000	750,000	0	Wendy
Bob's RRSP	1,000,000	750,000	1,000,000	Paul
Total Registered Assets	**2,000,000**	**1,500,000**	**1,000,000**	
Personal Use Assets				
Principal Residence	1,000,000	750,000	0	Wendy
Cottage	1,000,000	750,000	375,000	Paul
Total Personal Use Assets	**2,000,000**	**1,500,000**	**375,000**	
Total Estate Assets	**6,000,000**	**3,750,000**	**1,750,000**	

*Success Tax
Mary's Open - Taxed annually so therefore, no Success Tax
Bob's Open - $750,000 *50% Capital gain is taxable
Mary's TFSA - Exempt from taxation
Bob's RRSP - $1,000,000 fully taxable
Principal Residence - Exempt from taxation
Cottage - $750,000 *50% Capital gain is taxable

As you can see from the charts on the previous page, even though the assets all have the same fair market value (FMV) and the same adjusted cost base (ACB) and therefore the same amount of gains, the taxable gains depend on two things: what type of account the asset is held in and the kind of asset that it is.

Let's look at the three accounts that hold the ABC Stock, Bob's open, Bob's RRSP and Mary's TFSA. Even though all three of these accounts hold $1,000,000 of ABC stock, that they purchased for $250,000 each, the tax due is entirely different. The taxable amount on the RRSP is $1,000,000 while the taxable amount on Bob's open is just $375,000 (50% of the $750,000 capital gain) and there is $0 taxable on Mary's TFSA. Therefore, at an assumed 50% tax rate there is tax due on the RRSP of $500,000 while the tax due on Bob's open is $187,500 and there is $0 tax due on the TFSA. Three accounts that hold the same assets owe three different amounts of tax. This is due to the different tax treatments and how various types of accounts are taxed.

Chapter 13

As Dealt

For the first deal, we will assume the following. As in all of our examples, we will assume that Bob and Mary both pass away at the same time, and the values of the accounts are the same as in the examples on the previous pages. Bob has been talking to one of his friends about probate fees and is concerned about the fees that will be due upon his estate. He has found out that he can avoid probate by naming his son Paul as beneficiary on his RRSP, and as a joint owner of the cottage and his investment account. Bob adds Paul's name as the beneficiary on the RRSP and he makes Paul joint owner of the cottage, he also adds Paul's name to his investment account. Bob estimates this allows them to avoid about $45,000 in probate fees. By doing this Bob could have triggered the Success Tax as soon as he added Paul's name to the cottage and the investment account, however, I will ignore that risk in this example.

Now let's look at what happens when Bob and Mary pass away.

Smith Asset Details – As dealt

	Totals	Taxable	Success Tax Due*	Heir
Non-Registered Assets				
Mary's Open	1,000,000	0	0	Estate
Bob's Open	1,000,000	375,000	187,500	Paul
Total Non-Registered Assets	**2,000,000**	**375,000**	**187,500**	
Registered Assets				
Mary's TFSA	1,000,000	0		Estate
Bob's RRSP	1,000,000	1,000,000	500,000	Paul
Total Registered Assets	**2,000,000**	**1,000,000**	**500,000**	
Personal Use Assets				
Principal Residence	1,000,000	0		Estate
Cottage	1,000,000	375,000	187,500	Paul
Total Personal Use Assets	**2,000,000**	**375,000**	**187,500**	
Total Estate Assets	**6,000,000**	**2,500,000**	**875,000**	

*Success Tax Due
Bob's open – $750,000 * 50% taxable gain * 50% Tax
Bob's RRSP $1,000,000 * 50% Tax
Cottage $750,000 * 50% taxable gain * 50% Tax

Paul gets the $1,000,000 cottage, the $1,000,000 from the RRSP, and the $1,000,000 from Bob's investment account. Because Paul was made the joint owner or the beneficiary on all of these assets, the assets transfer directly over to him, outside of the estate and probate fees are avoided.

The Estate gets the $1,000,000 house, the $1,000,000 from the TFSA and the $1,000,000 from Mary's investment account. Before the estate can be settled it must go through probate. The probate on the estates $3,000,000 worth of assets is around $45,000. The Will clearly states that all of these assets are to go to Wendy, and since Paul already has his share of the estate these assets belong to Wendy. However, in order for the estate to be settled and in order for Wendy to get her money, the Success Tax must be paid. In this case, the Success Tax is estimated to be around $875,000. Made up of $500,000 of tax on the RRSP, $187,500 tax on the cottage and $187,500 tax on Bob's investment account. Just because these assets are not in the estate does not mean that the tax is not due. Therefore, before Wendy can get her money $915,000 ($875,000 tax + $45,000 probate) must be paid from the Estate.

Since Paul has already received his money, he has no interest in paying any of it back to the estate to cover the taxes due, and his new wife Donna convinces him not to as Donna has never really liked Wendy since Wendy is still good friends with Paul's first wife. Paul agrees with Donna as he doesn't want to cause any more problems in their already troubled marriage. This means that the money has to be paid out of the estate's $3,000,000. After the $915,000 in Success Tax and probate is paid, this leaves just $2,085,000 to be paid to Wendy.

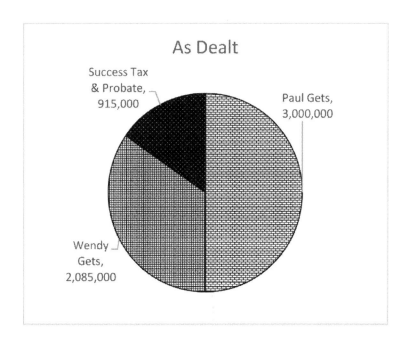

As Dealt

Success Tax & Probate, 915,000

Paul Gets, 3,000,000

Wendy Gets, 2,085,000

In this case, Paul and Wendy both end up with a house worth $1,000,000. But Paul gets $2,000,000 in cash and Wendy ends up with only $1,085,000, that is $915,000 less then Paul got. Surely this is not what Bob and Mary had intended, and certainly not worth the $45,000 Bob saved in estate fees by adding Paul's name to his accounts. Wendy can try to go after Paul for the money, but this could lead to a long drawn out battle, and there is no way to say for sure what would happen. Wendy is so mad at what Paul has done that they never talk again, and the families grow apart.

Chapter 14
Shuffle 1

That doesn't seem fair, so let's shuffle the deck and try this again.

For the first shuffle, we will assume the following. Bob & Mary have been talking to their friends about probate fees, and they are concerned about how this will affect their estate. They have been told that they can avoid probate with joint ownership and by naming their kids as beneficiaries on Bob's RRSP and Mary's TFSA, so they do this. They add both kids jointly to both of the properties, and both of the investment accounts. They estimate this allows them to avoid about $90,000 in probate fees. Again by making the kids joint owners Bob and Mary could be triggering the Success Tax, but once again we will ignore the risk in this example.

Now let's look at what happens when Bob and Mary pass away.

Smith Asset Details– Shuffle 1

	Totals	Taxable	Success Tax Due*	Heir
Non-Registered Assets				
Mary's Open	1,000,000	0	0	Joint
Bob's Open	1,000,000	375,000	187,500	Joint
Total Non-Registered Assets	**2,000,000**	**375,000**	**187,500**	
Registered Assets				
Mary's TFSA	1,000,000	0		Joint
Bob's RRSP	1,000,000	1,000,000	500,000	Joint
Total Registered Assets	**2,000,000**	**1,000,000**	**500,000**	
Personal Use Assets				
Principal Residence	1,000,000	0		Joint
Cottage	1,000,000	375,000	187,500	Joint
Total Personal Use Assets	**2,000,000**	**375,000**	**187,500**	
Total Estate Assets	**6,000,000**	**2,500,000**	**875,000**	

*Success Tax Due
Bob's open – $750,000 * 50% taxable gain * 50% Tax
Bob's RRSP $1,000,000 * 50% Tax
Cottage $750,000 * 50% taxable gain * 50% Tax

All of the assets are now jointly owned by Paul and Wendy. Because everything was jointly owned, all the assets transfer over outside of the Will and no probate fees are due.

According to Bob and Mary's wishes, Paul sells his share of the house to Wendy and Wendy sells her share of the cottage to Paul. At the same time Paul sells the cottage to his wife Donna. Remember Paul has creditor problems, and he doesn't want to risk losing the cottage to his creditors. He also transfers all of the cash accounts in his name to Donna at the same time and for the same reason.

With this shuffle there are no assets in the estate. However, just because the estate has no assets does not mean the Success Tax is not due. In this case, the Success Tax is still estimated to be around $875,000. Before the estate can be settled the taxes have to be paid from the estate. The estate still needs to be settled, even though it doesn't have any assets. Since the estate has no money the tax man will go after the new owners of the assets that use to be in Bob and Mary's names, and they do not care that the estate was split 50/50, they just want their share. So since Paul doesn't have any money nor assets in his name, as he transferred them all to his wife Donna, the tax man will go after Wendy.

Wendy pays the $875,000 in taxes out of her share of the estate, and hopes that Paul will pay her back. Since Paul doesn't have control of the assets anymore, as they are all in Donna's name, there is little chance that this is ever going to happen.

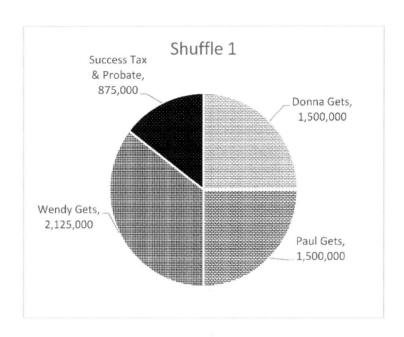

So when everything settles Paul's wife Donna and Wendy each end up with a house worth $1,000,000. However, Paul's wife Donna ends up with $2,000,000 in cash and Wendy is left with just $1,125,000, ($2,000,000 less the $875,000 in taxes).

So once again Wendy gets much less than her fair share of the estate, all for the sake of saving $90,000 in probate fees. Not what Bob and Mary wanted to happen.

In an odd twist of fate, Paul doesn't get away with this scot-free. Shortly after he puts all the assets into Donna's name, she files for divorce. Since the estate assets were put into his wife's name, they now form part of their Net Family Property and Donna is now entitled to 50% of these assets upon divorce. Had the assets remained only in

Paul's name they would not form part of their Net Family Property and Paul would have been protected. If he had left the assets in his name, he could likely have paid back his creditors and been in a much better place, than if he had not tried to save a few dollars by avoiding paying his debts.

Wendy is so mad at Paul that they never talk to each other again. After the divorce, Paul ends up with half of the assets from his share of the estate and Donna takes the other half. Paul has a $1,000,000 cottage that he can't afford to keep and $500,000 in cash, of which his creditors take their share. Surely, Bob and Mary are rolling over in their graves.

Chapter 15
Shuffle 2

Time to reshuffle. For the second shuffle, we will assume the following. Bob and Mary have heard of the possible risks of joint ownership, and because they think something is up with Paul and his wife they decide against adding the kids names to anything, not even as beneficiaries on the RRSP or TFSA.

Now let's look at what happens when Bob and Mary pass away.

Smith Asset Details – Shuffle 2

	Totals	Taxable	Success Tax Due*	Heir
Non-Registered Assets				
Mary's Open	1,000,000	0	0	Estate
Bob's Open	1,000,000	375,000	187,500	Estate
Total Non-Registered Assets	**2,000,000**	**375,000**	**187,500**	
Registered Assets				
Mary's TFSA	1,000,000	0		Estate
Bob's RRSP	1,000,000	1,000,000	500,000	Estate
Total Registered Assets	**2,000,000**	**1,000,000**	**500,000**	
Personal Use Assets				
Principal Residence	1,000,000	0		Estate
Cottage	1,000,000	375,000	187,500	Estate
Total Personal Use Assets	**2,000,000**	**375,000**	**187,500**	
Total Estate Assets	**6,000,000**	**2,500,000**	**875,000**	

*Success Tax Due
Bob's open – $750,000 * 50% taxable gain * 50% Tax
Bob's RRSP $1,000,000 * 50% Tax
Cottage $750,000 * 50% taxable gain * 50% Tax

All of the assets now form part of the estate and probate fees are due; these come to about $90,000. All of the liquid assets are sold, the Success Tax of $875,000 is paid. Paul gets the cottage and Wendy gets the house, and the estate is left with $3,035,000 to be split between Wendy and Paul.

Both Wendy and Paul get an equal share of the estate and continue to attend family gatherings together and enjoy the cottage with their children for the rest of their lives.

Paul gets some good advice from a financial planner and pays off his creditors and he keeps all of the estate assets in his own name. Now that Paul is no longer on the verge of going broke his wife Donna sees him in a different light and Paul and Donna stay married and their relationship continues to improve.

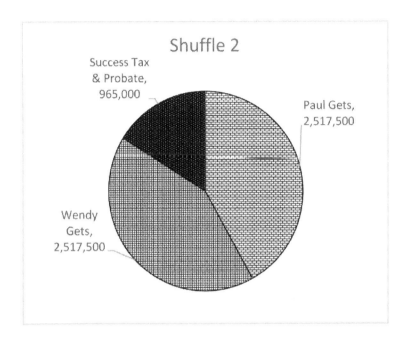

So, after all is said and done Paul and Wendy each end up with a house worth $1,000,000, and they both have $1,517,500 in cash. This is what Bob and Mary had wanted, all except for the $875,000 Success Tax bill.

Chapter 16
Shuffle 3

This still doesn't seem right. Let's shuffle the deck again and see if we can improve things a little more. For the third shuffle, we will assume the following. Bob & Mary have been told that they can avoid probate by naming their kids as beneficiaries on Bob's RRSP and Mary's TFSA, and that as long as the kids keep the money in their own names their spouses will not be able to get their hands on the money. They go ahead and make the kids beneficiaries on their RRSP and TFSA accounts. They estimate this allows them to avoid about $30,000 in probate fees.

Now let's look at what happens when Bob and Mary pass away.

Smith Asset Details – Shuffle 3

	Totals	Taxable	Success Tax Due*	Heir
Non-Registered Assets				
Mary's Open	1,000,000	0	0	Split
Bob's Open	1,000,000	375,000	187,500	Split
Total Non-Registered Assets	**2,000,000**	**375,000**	**187,500**	
Registered Assets				
Mary's TFSA	1,000,000	0		Wendy
Bob's RRSP	1,000,000	1,000,000	500,000	Paul
Total Registered Assets	**2,000,000**	**1,000,000**	**500,000**	
Personal Use Assets				
Principal Residence	1,000,000	0		Estate
Cottage	1,000,000	375,000	187,500	Estate
Total Personal Use Assets	**2,000,000**	**375,000**	**187,500**	
Total Estate Assets	**6,000,000**	**2,500,000**	**875,000**	

*Success Tax Due
Bob's open – $750,000 * 50% taxable gain * 50% Tax
Bob's RRSP $1,000,000 * 50% Tax
Cottage $750,000 * 50% taxable gain * 50% Tax

The RRSP transfers to Paul and the TFSA transfers to Wendy; all of the other assets form part of the estate.

The estate transfers the cottage to Paul and the house to Wendy. The $2,000,000 in the estate from the investment accounts is used to pay the probate fees of $60,000 and the Success Tax of $875,000. So the estate has $1,065,000 in cash that is equally divided between Wendy and Paul.

Paul talks to a financial planner, and he gets some great advice. He pays off his creditors and keeps all the money in his own name, and everyone lives happily ever after.

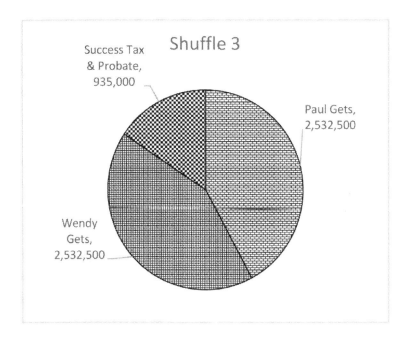

So after all is said and done Paul and Wendy each end up with a house worth $1,000,000, and $1,532,500 in cash each. Again this is what Bob and Mary had wanted, except for the $875,000 Success Tax payment.

Chapter 17
Shuffle 4

This is certainly getting better, but I think there is still room for improvement. For the fourth shuffle, we will assume the following. Once again Bob & Mary know that they can avoid some probate fees by naming their kids as beneficiaries on Bob's RRSP and Mary's TFSA, and that as long as the kids keep the money in their own names that their spouses will not be able to get their hands on the money. They go ahead and make the beneficiary designations. They estimate this allows them to avoid about $30,000 in probate fees.

This time, they decide that they want to make a donation to their favorite charity when they are gone. They both agree that they will leave the $1,000,000 from Mary's open nonregistered account to charity in their Wills, and have their Wills amended to show this.

Now let's look at what happens when Bob and Mary pass away.

Smith Asset Details – Shuffle 4

	Totals	Taxable	Success Tax Due*	Heir
Non-Registered Assets				
Mary's Open	1,000,000	0	0	Charity
Bob's Open	1,000,000	375,000	187,500	Estate
Total Non-Registered Assets	**2,000,000**	**375,000**	**187,500**	
Registered Assets				
Mary's TFSA	1,000,000	0		Wendy
Bob's RRSP	1,000,000	1,000,000	500,000	Paul
Total Registered Assets	**2,000,000**	**1,000,000**	**500,000**	
Personal Use Assets				
Principal Residence	1,000,000	0		Estate
Cottage	1,000,000	375,000	187,500	Estate
Total Personal Use Assets	**2,000,000**	**375,000**	**187,500**	
Charitable Donation	-1,000,000	-1,000,000	-400,000	
Total Estate Assets	**5,000,000**	**1,500,000**	**475,000**	

*Success Tax Due
Bob's open – $750,000 * 50% taxable gain * 50% Tax
Bob's RRSP $1,000,000 * 50% Tax
Cottage $750,000 * 50% taxable gain * 50% Tax
The $1,000,000 donation reduces the taxes due on the estate by $400,000 therefore the net cost to the estate was just $600,000

The RRSP transfers to Paul, and the TFSA transfers to Wendy and all of the other assets form part of the estate.

The estate transfers the cottage to Paul and the house to Wendy. The $1,000,000 from Mary's non-registered account is donated to charity, and the other $1,000,000 in the estate from Bob's investment account is used to pay the probate fees of around $60,000 and the Success Tax of $475,000. Notice now that the Success Tax is $400,000 lower than it was before; this is due to the tax credit for the charitable donation. So the estate has $465,000 left in cash after probate, the Success Tax, and the donation. This cash is equally divided between Wendy and Paul.

Again Paul gets some great advice from a financial planner and keeps all the assets in his own name; he pays off his creditors, and everyone lives happily ever after.

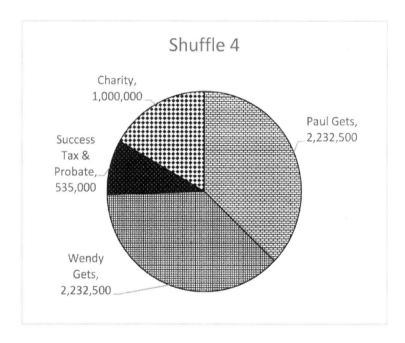

So after all is said and done Paul and Wendy both end up with a house worth $1,000,000, and $1,232,500 in cash each, and Bob and Mary's favorite charity gets $1,000,000. So in comparison to shuffle 3, the kids have ended up with $300,000 less each, but the tax man gets $400,000 less, and the charity gets $1,000,000 more. All around not a bad deal.

Chapter 18
Shuffle 5

I think we are starting to get somewhere. For the fifth shuffle, we will assume the following. Once again Bob & Mary know that they can avoid probate by naming their kids as beneficiaries on Bob's RRSP and Mary's TFSA, and that as long as the kids keep the money in their own names that their spouses will not be able to get their hands on the money. They go ahead and make the beneficiary designations. They estimate this allows them to avoid about $30,000 in probate fees.

Again they have decided that they want to make a donation to their favorite charity when they are gone. However, this time, they are going to leave the $1,000,000 of ABC Stock from Bob's open nonregistered account to charity. This will be done in their will as an in-kind transfer, as they have heard that there are some tax benefits to a donation of a publicly traded security to a charity. They amend their Wills to reflect their wishes.

Now let's look at what happens when Bob and Mary pass away.

Smith Asset Details – Shuffle 5

	Totals	Taxable	Success Tax Due*	Heir
Non-Registered Assets				
Mary's Open	1,000,000	0	0	Estate
Bob's Open	1,000,000	0	0	Charity
Total Non-Registered Assets	**2,000,000**	**0**	**0**	
Registered Assets				
Mary's TFSA	1,000,000	0		Wendy
Bob's RRSP	1,000,000	1,000,000	500,000	Paul
Total Registered Assets	**2,000,000**	**1,000,000**	**500,000**	
Personal Use Assets				
Principal Residence	1,000,000	0		Estate
Cottage	1,000,000	375,000	187,500	Estate
Total Personal Use Assets	**2,000,000**	**375,000**	**187,500**	
Charitable Donation	-1,000,000	-1,000,000	-400,000	
Total Estate Assets	**5,000,000**	**0**	**287,500**	

*Success Tax Due
Bob's open – By making an in kind donation of the publicly traded ABC Stock, Bob's estate does not have to claim the capital gain on the sale of the stock, saving the estate $187,500 in taxes
Bob's RRSP $1,000,000 * 50% Tax
Cottage $750,000 * 50% taxable gain * 50% Tax
The $1,000,000 donation reduces the taxes due on the estate by $400,000 and with the $187,500 saved by not having to claim the capital gain the net cost to the estate was just $412,500

The RRSP transfers to Paul, and the TFSA transfers to Wendy and all of the other assets form part of the estate.

The estate transfers the cottage to Paul and the house to Wendy. The $1,000,000 from Bob's non-registered account is donated directly to the charity in-kind (as ABC Stock), and the $1,000,000 in Mary's investment account is used to pay the probate fees of $60,000 and the Success Tax of $287,500. I told you this was looking better, notice the Success Tax is now $587,500 lower than in shuffles one, two and three and $187,500 lower than in shuffle four. This is because of two things: the tax credit from the donation and not having to include the $750,000 capital gain on Bob's ABC shares. This happens because when you donate certain capital assets to charity, you are not required to claim the capital gain on those assets. So the estate now has $652,500 in cash left that is equally divided between Wendy and Paul.

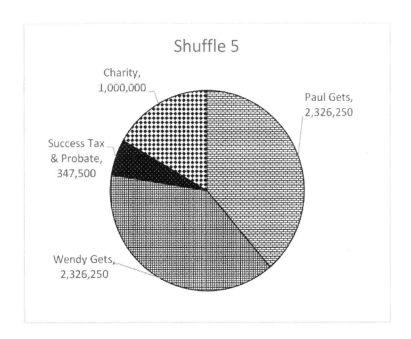

After all is said and done Paul and Wendy both end up with a house worth $1,000,000, and $1,326,250 in cash each, and Bob and Mary's favorite charity gets $1,000,000. That means that Paul and Wendy both get only $206,250 less than in shuffle 3, the tax man gets $587,500 less, and the charity gets $1,000,000.

Again Paul pays off his creditors, and gets some great advice and keeps all the assets in his own name, and everyone lives happily ever after.

Chapter 19
Shuffle 6

This is starting to look much better. For the sixth shuffle, we will assume the following. Once again Bob & Mary know that they can avoid probate by naming their kids as beneficiaries on Bob's RRSP and Mary's TFSA, and that as long as the kids keep the money in their own names that their spouses will not be able to get their hands on the money. They go ahead and make the beneficiary designations. They estimate this allows them to avoid about $30,000 in probate fees.

Once again they have decided that they want to make a donation to their favorite charity after they are gone. As in shuffle five, they are going to leave the $1,000,000 of ABC Stock from Bob's open nonregistered account to charity in their will as an in-kind transfer, due to the tax benefits of a donation of publicly traded securities to a charity. They have their Wills amended to reflect this.

This time, to ensure that they do not deplete the value of their estate because of the donation they are going to purchase a joint last to die Estate Preservation Life Insurance Plan *(See chapter 22 for details on how an EPLIP works)*. They are going to pay for the policy with the 3% dividends from Bob's ABC stock in his open nonregistered account. The dividend is $30,000 a year before taxes and the policy cost is around $20,000 per year and provides the estate with a $1,000,000 tax-free benefit upon the last death. They name Paul and Wendy as beneficiaries of the estate preservation plan; this means the money will pass to them outside of the estate and it will not be subject to probate.

Now let's look at what happens when Bob and Mary pass away.

Smith Asset Details – Shuffle 6

	Totals	Taxable	Success Tax Due*	Heir
Non-Registered Assets				
Mary's Open	1,000,000	0	0	Estate
Bob's Open	1,000,000	0	0	Charity
Total Non-Registered Assets	**2,000,000**	**0**	**0**	
Registered Assets				
Mary's TFSA	1,000,000	0		Wendy
Bob's RRSP	1,000,000	1,000,000	500,000	Paul
Total Registered Assets	**2,000,000**	**1,000,000**	**500,000**	
Personal Use Assets				
Principal Residence	1,000,000	0		Estate
Cottage	1,000,000	375,000	187,500	Estate
Total Personal Use Assets	**2,000,000**	**375,000**	**187,500**	
Charitable Donation	-1,000,000	-1,000,000	-400,000	
Estate Preservation Plan	1,000,000	0	0	Split
Total Estate Assets	**7,000,000**	**0**	**287,500**	

*Success Tax Due
The proceeds from the Estate Preservation Plan are tax and probate free.
Bob's open – By making an in kind donation of the publicly traded ABC Stock, Bob's estate does not have to claim the capital gain on the sale of the stock, saving the estate $187,500 in taxes
Bob's RRSP $1,000,000 * 50% Tax
Cottage $750,000 * 50% taxable gain * 50% Tax
The $1,000,000 donation reduces the taxes due on the estate by $400,000 and with the $187,500 saved by not having to claim the capital gain the net cost to the estate was just $412,500

Since Wendy and Paul are the beneficiaries of the insurance policy, the payment is made directly to Wendy and Paul. This means that it does not form part of the estate. Since insurance proceeds are not subject to taxation, Wendy and Paul each get $500,000 tax and probate free.

The RRSP transfers to Paul, and the TFSA transfers to Wendy and all of the other assets form part of the estate.

The estate transfers the cottage to Paul and the house to Wendy. The $1,000,000 from Bob's non-registered investment account is donated directly to charity in-kind as ABC Stock, and the $1,000,000 in Mary's investment account is used to pay the probate fees of $60,000 and the Success Tax of $287,500. This is the same Success Tax as in shuffle 5, but it is still $587,500 lower than before because of the tax credit from the donation and not having to include the $750,000 capital gain on Bob's ABC shares. This time, the estate has $652,500 in cash that is equally divided between Wendy and Paul.

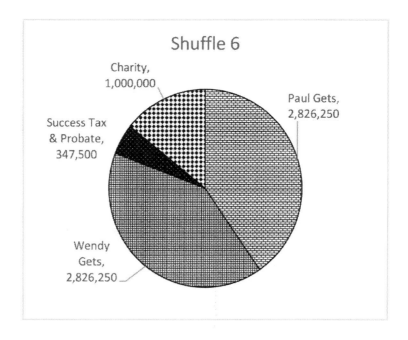

After all is said and done Paul and Wendy each end up with a house worth $1,000,000, and $1,826,250 in cash, and Bob and Mary's favorite charity gets $1,000,000. With this shuffle each of the kids gets $500,000 more than they did in shuffle five because of the insurance policy. The cost to the Smiths was just $20,000 per year which was paid from the dividend from Bobs open investment account.

Again Paul gets some great advice and keeps all the assets in his own name, and everyone lives happily ever after.

Chapter 20
Shuffle 7

Ok, let's try this one more time. For the seventh shuffle, we will assume the following. Once again Bob and Mary know that they can avoid probate by naming their kids as beneficiaries on Bob's RRSP and Mary's TFSA, and that as long as the kids keep the money in their own names that their spouses will not be able to get their hands on the money. They go ahead and make the beneficiary designations. They estimate this allows them to avoid about $30,000 in probate fees.

As in shuffles five and six, they are going to make a donation to their favorite charity, once they are gone. As before they are going to leave the $1,000,000 of ABC Stock from Bob's open non-registered investment account. In addition, this time, they are going to leave an extra $875,000 from Mary's non-registered account to charity as well. These donations will be made in their Will.

As with shuffle six, to ensure that they do not deplete the value of their estate too much because of the donations they are going to purchase a joint last to die Estate Preservation Life Insurance Plan *(See chapter 22 for details on how an EPLIP works)*. They are going to pay for the policy with the 3% dividends from Bob's ABC stock held in his open nonregistered account. The dividend is $30,000 a year before taxes, and the policy cost is around $ 20,000 annually. They name Paul and Wendy as beneficiaries of the estate preservation plan.

Now let's look at what happens when Bob and Mary pass away.

Smith Asset Details – Shuffle 7

	Totals	Taxable	Success Tax Due*	Heir
Non-Registered Assets				
Mary's Open	1,000,000	0	0	Split
Bob's Open	1,000,000	0	0	Charity
Total Non-Registered Assets	**2,000,000**	**0**	**0**	
Registered Assets				
Mary's TFSA	1,000,000	0		Wendy
Bob's RRSP	1,000,000	1,000,000	500,000	Paul
Total Registered Assets	**2,000,000**	**1,000,000**	**500,000**	
Personal Use Assets				
Principal Residence	1,000,000	0		Wendy
Cottage	1,000,000	375,000	187,500	Paul
Total Personal Use Assets	**2,000,000**	**375,000**	**187,500**	
Charitable Donation	-1,375,000	-1,375,000	-552,000	
Charitable Donation**	-500,000	-500,000	-200,000	
Estate Preservation Plan	1,000,000	0	0	Split
Total Estate Assets	**7,000,000**	**0**	**-64,500**	

*Success Tax Due
The proceeds from the Estate Preservation Plan are tax and probate free.
Bob's open – By making an in kind donation of the publicly traded ABC Stock, Bob's estate does not have to claim the capital gain on the sale of the stock, saving the estate $187,500 in taxes
Bob's RRSP $1,000,000 * 50% Tax
Cottage $750,000 * 50% taxable gain * 50% Tax
**Since the total donation is greater than the taxable income $500,000 of the donation is carried back for the previous tax year in order to get back taxes that have already been paid. This totally offsets the Success of $687,500 and leaves an extra $64,500 to cover the probate fees.

As the named beneficiaries the insurance payment is made directly to Wendy and Paul and this means that it does not form part of the estate. Since insurance proceeds are not subject to taxation, Paul and Wendy each get $500,000 tax and probate free.

The RRSP transfers to Paul, and the TFSA transfers to Wendy and all of the other assets form part of the estate.

The estate transfers the cottage to Paul and the house to Wendy. The $1,000,000 from Bob's non-registered investment account is donated directly to charity in-kind (as ABC Stock), and $875,000 from Mary's investment account is used to make an additional donation. The remaining $125,000 from Mary's account is used to pay the probate fees of $60,000.

Now, as is the case in this example, if Bob and Mary have no other taxable income in the year of death, the total donation of $1,875,000 would be $500,000 over the allowable deduction limit on their final tax returns. This would mean that the estate would only get to deduct $1,375,000 of the donation, as you cannot deduct more than 100% of the taxable income on your final tax return. Therefore, the estate would still owe $135,500 in taxes. However, their estate would be allowed to carry back the excess $500,000 donation to the previous tax year. Carrying back the excess donation would result in a refund of $200,000 which would entirely offset the Success Tax, of $135,500 as well as the $60,000 in probate fees that the estate paid.

With this additional refund, the Success Tax along with the probate fee has been eliminated, due to this shuffle.

Charity $1,875,000 - CRA $0.

This is due to the tax credits from the charitable donations and not having to include the $750,000 capital gain on Bob's ABC shares.

Once all the tax returns are filed, and the refunds are issued, along with the cash left from Mary's investment account, the estate would have around $125,000. This would be equally divided between Wendy and Paul.

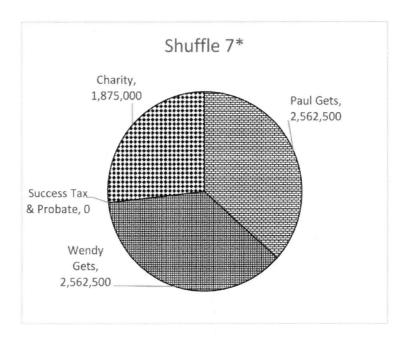

After all is said and done Paul and Wendy each end up with a house worth $1,000,000, and $1,562,500 in cash, and Bob and Mary's favorite charity gets $1,875,000. So a total of $7,000,000 gets paid out from a $6,000,000 estate, and the tax man gets nothing. As you will notice with this shuffle Paul and Wendy both end up with $263,750 less than in shuffle 6, however, the charity ends up with $875,000 more and the tax man gets $347,500 less. All in all not a bad deal.

Again Paul gets some great advice pays his debts and keeps all the assets in his own name, and everyone lives happily ever after.

Chapter 21
Shuffle Summary

The shuffles on the previous pages are by no means the only options available to Bob and Mary. With proper planning there are many ways that Bob and Mary can protect their heirs and reduce the Success Tax on their estate. They just need to become acutely aware of exactly how their estate is going to be or could be affected by the choices that they make.

Summarized in the charts on the next page are the different outcomes of the shuffles we did for Bob and Mary. By making the charitable donations, they have managed to entirely disinherit CRA and reduce their Success Tax to $0. By purchasing the EPLIP, they have also been able to make the donations without affecting the amount of money that they were able to leave behind to Paul and Wendy.

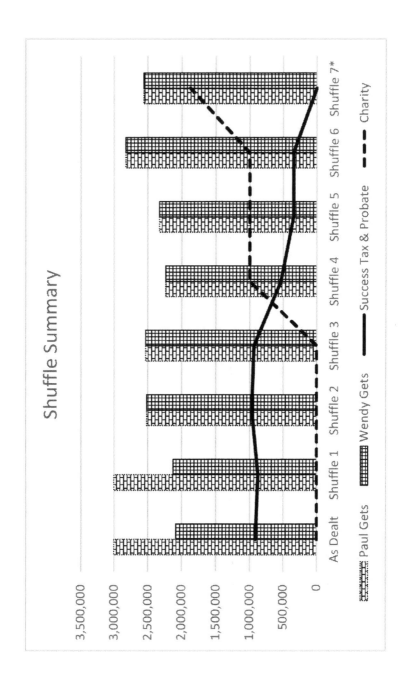

Shuffle Summary

	Paul Gets	**Wendy Gets**	**Success Tax & Probate**	**Charity**
As Dealt	3,000,000	2,085,000	915,000	0
Shuffle 1	3,000,000	2,125,000	875,000	0
Shuffle 2	2,517,500	2,517,500	965,000	0
Shuffle 3	2,532,500	2,532,500	935,000	0
Shuffle 4	2,232,500	2,232,500	535,000	1,000,000
Shuffle 5	2,326,250	2,326,250	347,500	1,000,000
Shuffle 6	2,826,250	2,826,250	347,500	1,000,000
Shuffle 7*	2,562,500	2,562,500	0	1,875,000

* The donation in shuffle 7 is greater than the taxable income therefore, part of the donation is carried back to the previous tax year, inorder to get back taxes that have already been paid. This additonal refund will totally offset the Success Tax and the probate fee.

As you can see, there are many options available to Bob and Mary, all with different financial outcomes.

In my examples we have assumed that Bob and Mary both pass away at the same time and that their accounts all have the same market values and underlying ACBs. However, we know that this never happens in real life. Assets are rarely equal and usually one person would pass away first, and then all the assets would roll over to the remaining spouse on a tax-deferred basis. With proper estate planning, upon the death of the second spouse the net income in the year of death plus the allowable carryback to the previous year, should be more than enough to allow a full deduction for the donation, as it was with shuffle 7. The resulting refunds should entirely offset the Success Tax and the probate fees.

Also, Bob and Mary would hopefully never hold a portfolio that is so concentrated in one holding. It is hazardous to have not only 50% of your employment income determined by one company but to have 50% of your investments dependent on that company as well. Diversification and asset allocation are key to successful money management.

As stated, tax rates and credits vary from province to province. The examples in this book are simplified examples of a complicated situation; please seek personalized professional guidance with your estate and tax planning. Work with someone who has the knowledge and experience to give you the advice you need and who knows you, your family, your goals and your objectives, before acting. Working with a personal financial and estate planner can help you minimize the Success Tax and maximize the benefits to your heirs and favorite charities.

Chapter 22

Estate Preservation Life Insurance Plans

An Estate Preservation Life Insurance Plan (EPLIP) is just one option that can be used to help you and your family with your estate planning goals. In some cases, it is a simple, affordable option and it works very well; in others it is simply not the right option. It is, however, one of the general public's least understood options. That is why I decided to include it as the last chapter in this book.

There are many types, options, bells and whistles that can be used in an EPLIP, and it is not possible to explain all of them in this book, so I will only try and highlight a few. You need to work with someone who understands EPLIPs and who you trust to find out if this option is right for you and your family.

An EPLIP is a life insurance policy that is taken out with the intent of using the proceeds in the estate of the insured. The proceeds can be utilized for any purpose. The most common would be:

Estate Equalization: making sure there is enough cash in the estate to treat all heirs equally, often used by business owners when they do not leave the business to all family members. Or when a family cottage or rental property is left to one child, and cash is to be left to other members.

Debt Repayment: having an EPLIP in place means that the insured could go into debt during their lifetime, and use the proceeds of the insurance to eliminate the debt on their death.

Charitable Donation: donating annual amounts to your favorite charity is always a good thing. However, being able to help out by leaving behind a larger donation that you might have otherwise not have been able to make helps out your favorite charity even more. And it has the added advantage of reducing your Success Tax when planned properly.

Success Tax payment: you have seen just how big of a bite the Success Tax could take out of your estate, so having an EPLIP in place to ensure that there is enough liquid cash to make this payment, can be a great estate planning tool. Especially in situations where liquidity of estate assets is an issue. This often happens with family businesses and family cottages.

Family Wealth Transfer: often an EPLIP is used to ensure the tax-effective transfer of wealth down to the next generation or even to the generation after that;

EPLIPs offer flexibility when it comes to estate planning as you could put a plan in place today to protect the family business or cottage and years from now your situation could change. You may end up selling the business or the cottage, and paying the taxes at the time of the sale.

This could mean that your estate no longer has a large Success Tax bill pending. If this is the case you could, then redirect the proceeds of the EPLIP to something else. If the EPLIP had a cash surrender value, you might just want to cash it out and use the funds for another purpose. Or you might want to make a larger donation to your favorite charity, or leave more for your heirs. The value that you had put into the plan is not lost, as it might be with some other estate planning methods. EPLIPs are one of the most flexible and cost-effective estate planning tools that exist.

An EPLIP is usually a whole life or permanent life insurance policy insuring one or more people. Since the policy needs to be in place when you die, the plan needs to cover you for your whole life as opposed to a plan that covers you if you die prematurely. If you are looking for coverage for an 'if you die prematurely situation', then a term insurance policy is a great product, with lower premiums and higher coverage. These plans are ideal for covering off short term or temporary needs, such as income replacement or debt repayment. However, as you get older, these plans become unaffordable and are not great options when it comes to the Success Tax or long-term estate planning. For long term planning, you need to use some form of whole life insurance, insurance that covers you for your whole life; there are several options here depending on your situation.

The simplest form of an EPLIP is Term to 100, which offers you straight life insurance, no cash value or dividends, and you pay your premiums for your whole life. The next would be a Whole Life policy that offers a cash value and dividends and the possibility of premium holidays. Lastly, there are Universal Life Policies which offer a multitude of investment choices and variable premium options, including quick pay and limited payment periods. What is right for you will depend on your personal situation and is something to discuss with your financial planner and licensed insurance advisor.

The one element that is often unique with an EPLIP is that because these policies are designed to cover off the expenses that occur to the estate the insurance payout happens upon the last death. Since most of these estate costs can be delayed or transferred to your spouse upon the first death, what is known as a Joint Last to Die policy is often used. This means that the insurance company insures both parties in a couple and that they do not usually pay out any death benefits until the last person dies. This allows the policy to be written up using what is known as the single equivalent age. This means that it is less expensive to purchase one policy covering the last death of two people than it would be to purchase a policy on just the younger person, this happens because the combined life expectancy of both people is greater than the life expectancy of the younger person. This dramatically reduces the overall cost of the insurance.

EPLIPs are often more affordable than people think. Also, an EPLIP with a tax-sheltered investment account inside of it shelters the money inside of the plan from taxation. If the investment inside of the plan is large enough, sometimes the premium payment required is less than what the tax would be on the investment if the investment was not sheltered inside of the EPLIP. When this happens the cost of the EPLIP is totally covered by the tax savings.

Using an EPLIP to pay your Success Tax can be a very cost-effective method of making this payment. In our examples, Bob and Mary are being very philanthropic and are using their donations to offset the Success Tax of $875,000. However, they could also just decide to use the proceeds of the EPLIP to pay the taxes, without making a donation. If they did this, the cost to them would be just the $20,000 a year until the last death, so even if one of them lived for 40 more years, the total cost (ignoring the time value of money) would be just $800,000, and their estate would end up with $1,000,000. Without the EPLIP, the estate could write a cheque to CRA for $875,000 and get a nice thank you letter in the mail. With the EPLIP Bob and Mary (or the kids benefiting from this) pay $20,000 a year. Upon the last death, the kids would receive a cheque from the insurance company for $1,000,000. They could use this to pay the $875,000 and end up with $125,000 left over plus they still get a thank you letter from CRA.

Which would you rather have come out of your bank account?

Bob and Mary Smith 123 Anystreet Anytown, ON		115
	Date *6 Months from ?*	
PAY TO THE ORDER OF	*Canada Revenue Agency*	$ 875,000.00
	Eight hundred and seventy five thousand - - xx /100 DOLLARS	
[$]	YOUR BANK 321 Main St. Anytown, ON	
Memo	*Success Tax payment*	*Your Executor* *from the estate of Bob & Mary Smith*
115	00089 00999 700589576	

Or

```
Bob and Mary Smith                                                                    105
123 Anystreet
Anytown, ON                                              Date  Annually

PAY TO THE            ABC Insurance Company                    $    20,000.00
ORDER OF           Twenty thousand - - - - - - - - - - - - - - - - - - xx /100 DOLLARS

        $        YOUR BANK
                 321 Main St.
                 Anytown, ON
Memo             $1,000,000 Tax free benefit          Bob & Mary Smith

     105      00089     00999    700589576
```

Do not assume that you are too old or uninsurable and that you can't purchase an EPLIP, as often people that think they are uninsurable or too old find that they are still eligible for this type of coverage. Sometimes even if one spouse or partner is totally uninsurable an EPLIP can still be a viable solution. It costs nothing, other than your time to find out if this is a solution that might work for you and your family. Contact your financial planner or insurance professional to see if an EPLIP would be a useful estate planning tool for you and your heirs.

My Goals

My first goal in writing this book is to help the general public gain a better understanding of just exactly what the Success Tax is, and what it could cost their estate, and to encourage them to take action to reduce the amount of Success Tax that their estate pays.

My second goal is to increase the amount of charitable donations that are being made from estates. We often think of our favorite charities annually with small regular donations. However, many people do not give much thought to what happens when they are gone, and their donations stop.

Charitable donations from your estate are an excellent way to reduce your Success Tax bill, and with all the program cutbacks that have happened in recent years our favorite charities need our support more than ever.

My third goal is to be directly or indirectly responsible for redirecting $1,000,000,000 (yes one billion dollars) of Success Tax to Charity. Therefore, if you and your estate planner have used the ideas in this book to reduce your Success Tax by allocating a donation from part of your estate to charity, I would like to ask you to please drop me a line and let me know just how much you have reduced your Success Tax by and what your donation amount will be.

I can be reached by email at wegreen@billgreen.ca or through my website at www.billgreen.ca

About the Author

William (Bill) Green has been in the financial and estate planning business for over 25 years. He is a Certified Financial Planner (CFP), Financial Management Advisor (FMA), and a Financial Divorce Specialist (FDS). He also holds his Chartered Investment Manager (CIM) designation and is one of only a handful of Canadians who is a member of the Nazrudin Project, an international advisory think-tank of financial planners, psychologists and other professionals dealing with the emotional and psychological aspects of money and money management.

Since he started in the financial services industry, he has worked for both small and large independent firms and with a large Canadian bank brokerage and their retail banking division. He now works as an independent advisor and consultant. He currently provides insurance solutions, fee only, hourly financial and estate planning advice to his clients and other advisors from his home in Muskoka, Ontario. He enjoys many outdoor activities including canoeing, kayaking, fishing, hiking, cross-country and downhill skiing. He can be reached through his website at www.billgreen.ca

Made in the USA
Columbia, SC
03 September 2017